CHESAPEAKE & OHIO
2-8-4 STEAM LOCOMOTIVES

By Thomas W. Dixon, Jr.

D1716087

Introduction to the Chesapeake & Ohio History Series Books Concept

This is the first in a series of softbound books we plan to publish on a quarterly basis. Each will have a particular C&O subject that, for some reason, has not been published in this detail in our magazine. The subject matter will have a wide range: steam and diesel locomotives; passenger and freight cars, operations of all types, structures and facilities of all kinds, histories of particular areas of the line such as a city, yard, or subdivision, and so forth. Readers are encouraged to make recommendations. Although we plan to issue these on a regular basis we are considering them books and not periodicals.

To subscribe to this series go to the chessieshop.com web site cited below.

The Society may be contacted by writing:

The Chesapeake & Ohio Historical Society, Inc.
312 East Ridgeway Street
Clifton Forge, VA 24422

or calling 1-540-862-2210 (Monday-Saturday 9am-5pm), or by e-mail at: cohs@cohs.org
The Society maintains a history information Internet site at
www.cohs.org, and a full service sales site at www.chessieshop.com.

For information on The C&O Railway Heritage Center visit www.candoheritage.org

Copy Editor: Rick Van Horn
Digital Production: Michael A. Dixon
Layout and Design: Michael A. Dixon and Mac Beard

International Standard Book Number 978-0-939487-59-2
Library of Congress Control Number 2013933889

ON THE COVER: C&O K-4 No. 2780 possibly near Selma Yard, Va. circa 1950. Photograph by Jack Manner. (C&OHS Collection, COHS 36926)

Table of Contents

Chapter One   *Genesis of the Kanawha Type on the C&O* ——— 5

Chapter Two   *Mechanical Specifications of the K-4 Class 2-8-4* —— 15

Chapter Three *Gene Huddleston on the K-4* ——————— 29

Chapter Four   *K-4s in Operation 1944-1956* ——————— 41

Chapter Five   *The "Other" C&O 2-8-4s* ——————— 75

K-4s Postscript *Afterlife* ———————————— 79

Introduction:

The C&O began to acquire its K-4 class 2-8-4 Kanawha type locomotives in 1943 and after the last order in 1949, it rostered 90 locomotives. Twenty of which were from C&O's then favored builder, Lima Locomotive Works, the remainder coming from American Locomotive Company's Schenectady Works.

The K-4s were not the only 2-8-4 types that appeared on the C&O steam locomotive roster. In 1947, when the Pere Marquette Railway was merged into the C&O, its 2-8-4s were incorporated into the C&O's fleet, adding 39 more of the type. The ex-PM engines, classed N through N-2 and originally built between 1937 and 1944, were not widely used on the old C&O lines and were soon displaced in Michigan by the rapid dieselization of the PM routes. Most of the C&O K-4s remained in service until the last years of steam, retiring in the 1952-1956 era.

The K-4 class has the distinction of being the largest class of C&O locomotives, and one of the largest class of any steam locomotive in America saved from scrap and preserved to modern times. This was because C&O's public relations department established a program to donate steam locomotives to museums and cities for display. The K-4 was the type most often chosen for donation, and 13 were saved. Twelve are still in existence as of this writing (2013).

The 2-8-4 type was introduced by Lima Locomotive Works in 1924 as the first of their new concept "Super Power" locomotives. The type was quickly named Berkshire after the mountains in New York over which the 2-8-4 was first tested and later used in regular service by the Boston & Albany Railroad, who did much of its testing. However, the class was given several other names by the various railroads that used it in the subsequent decades. C&O decided that with its southern roots (Richmond headquarters and Virginia nativity) a more appropriate name was required and thus called it Kanawha after the river, (also a county, and C&O subdivision) in West Virginia along whose banks the locomotives were frequently used.

The K-4 was a powerful and quite versatile locomotive type on the C&O and was used in a wide variety of service over a large portion of the system. They were used for fast freights, mainline coal trains, branch line coal trains, local freights, and even passenger trains. Indeed, in the era 1943-1948, they were in frequent passenger service because of the heavy war-time and immediate post-war traffic and the lack of available passenger power (that did not arrive until 1948).

Because of their versatility and ability to operate in most areas, they were among the last C&O steam locomotives retired, operating into the summer of 1956, when all steam operations ended. But even at that, the eldest of the class were only a decade old and the newest only five or six years–lives foreshortened by the abrupt turn to diesels.

Today, the K-4 is one of the iconic C&O modern Super Power locomotives, beloved of modelers and railfans alike. Only one was ever used in excursion service however, and it was disguised as a Southern Railway engine as part of the Southern's steam excursion program–No. 2716. It was returned to C&O appearance and resides today at the Kentucky Railway Museum.

This book is intended to give a general history of the dozen years of K-4 operation and to illustrate them in some detail. We hope you enjoy reading this volume as much as we enjoyed preparing it for you.

Thomas W. Dixon, Jr.

Clifton Forge, Va., January, 2013

CHAPTER ONE

Genesis of the Kanawha Type on the C&O

Though the C&O was the linchpin of the Van Sweringen railroad empire, it was the last of the Van Sweringen roads to acquire the 2-8-4 wheel arrangement. The family of 2-8-4s built for the Erie, Nickel Plate Road, Pere Marquette and finally C&O, became known as the "Van Sweringen Berkshires" because of their similarities (some parts were even interchangeable) and their ownership by the railroads under the Van Sweringen financial control. The Erie 2-8-4s, which began the line, were actually built before the Van Sweringens established a centralization of equipment design, but served as a model for the rest of the Van's Super Power.

The Cleveland real estate tycoons O. P. and M. J. Van Sweringen began putting together a conglomerate of railroads when they acquired the Nickel Plate Road (New York, Chicago & St. Louis) in 1916. They gained control of the C&O in 1923, along with its subsidiary Hocking Valley Railway, and they bought control of the Pere Marquette in 1928. The Erie came into their control in 1926. These roads constituted the core of the Van Sweringen railroad empire, though it had large interests in several other lines.

In an effort to standardize some practices among the independent lines (that remained so because of competition encouraged by laws and the regulation of the Interstate Commerce Commission), the Vans (as they were called) in 1929 established an "Advisory Mechanical Committee" (AMC) at their Cleveland headquarters. The AMC was to develop new equipment for the constituent railroads, standardize parts and designs across the companies, and generally achieve not only a degree of standardization, but of best practice for each of the lines.(see page 10). It was under this committee's guidance that the Van Sweringen Berkshires were refined and promoted.

The Lima #A-1 was the first 2-8-4 and established the type along with the Super Power concept which the C&O was to embrace in the last 25 years of steam. It was tested and used by Boston & Albany which gave the 2-8-4 its "Berkshire" name. (C&OHS Collection, COHS 36796)

The great Erie Railroad Class S 2-8-4 was the direct ancestor of most of the C&O's Super Power fleet, and in particular the T-1 2-0-4 and the K-4 2-8-4. It had 70-inch rivers, 72,000 lbs. tractive effort (85,000 with booster), 250 psi pressure, 100 sq. ft. of grate area, total engine weight of 457,500 lbs. and heating surface of 5,697 sq. in. (C&OHS Collection, COHS 36797)

The first of the 2-8-4s to come to the Van Sweringen roads was the Erie S class, arriving in September 1927. The subsequent fleet eventually amounted to 105 locomotives. They proved superbly useful in modernizing the Erie. A few years later the Erie 2-8-4 design prototype was used by the AMC, which enlarged it and used it as the basis for the C&O's T-1 class 2-10-4, the first of C&O's Super Power fleet. The C&O was so pleased with the T-1s and the whole Super Power idea that almost all the locomotives it bought thereafter to the end of steam were in this concept, and 61% of them were built by Super Power's progenitor, Lima Locomotive Works.

The next Van Sweringen road to get the 2-8-4 was the Nickel Plate in 1934. It eventually rostered four classes constituting 65 locomotives. NKP 2-8-4 No. 779 was the last Super Power locomotive commercially built in America, in 1949. The NKP S class 2-8-4 was essentially the result of the AMC downsizing the C&O T-1 2-10-4. Thus, the Erie class S begat the C&O T-1, which begat the NKP class S: 2-8-4 to 2-10-4 back to 2-8-4. The NKP locomotives were

arguably the most famous of the type and were magnificently used in fast freight service, but owe part of their fame to their late use, into 1957.

The Pere Marquette Railway of Michigan and Ontario came into the Van Sweringen orbit in 1928. In 1937, it received the benefit of AMC's locomotive designing when it was given its N class 2-8-4s. They were virtual duplicates of the NKP locomotives, which had been proving themselves so well since 1934. PM eventually had 39 locomotives in three sub-classes. They were the backbone of the PM's fast freight business, especially during World War II, and became part of the C&O fleet when PM was merged in 1947.

The Vans got control of C&O in 1923 as part of their "Greater Nickel Plate" plan, but with its burgeoning coal business C&O soon became the key player in the system. The AMC gave C&O its first Super Power design with the T-1 2-10-4s of 1930. This was followed by 4-8-4s in 1935 (J-3 class), and the magnificent H-8 class 2-6-6-6 Alleghenies of 1942, L-2 Hudsons in 1943, and then the 2-8-4s in

The fabulous C&O T-1 2-10-4 Texas type of 1930 was an enlargement of an Erie S-2. The T-1 was the ultimate non-articulated Super Power locomotive, and pleased C&O so much it bought little else but Super Power, and Lima Super Power in particular, to the end of steam. (C&OHS Collection, COHS 36798)

The Nickel Plate Road's 2-8-4s of 1934 were created by downsizing a C&O T-1 by the Van Sweringen's Advisory Mechanical Committee mechanical engineers. (C&OHS Collection, COHS 36799)

1943, C&O's famous K-4 class, about which this story revolves. Why the delay in getting the standard Van Sweringen freight power to the most important line in the system? Probably, and we can only guess, this was because C&O acquired in 1923-25 a group of about 150 very powerful, highly developed, well-designed, and quite versatile 2-8-2 Mikados (K-2, K-3 and K-3a classes). These were such good engines that there was no reason to supplement them until World War II traffic forced the issue. At least, this is the best conclusion from the scant information we have available. It's interesting to note that the class assigned to the 2-8-4s was the next after the last 2-8-2s: K-4. Also, many of the enginemen called the Kanawhas "Big Mikes," in recognition of their carrying on in the manner of the Mikados.

In an unusual twist, the Virginian Railway, one of the two C&O competitors for transportation of coal to the Hampton Roads ports, had Lima build five virtual duplicates to the C&O K-4s, which it classed BA, and called them Berkshires. Except for the lettering and a few minor changes they look almost exactly like C&O K-4s, the difference being that the steam dome and sandbox were combined in one housing

similar to that used on C&O's J-3A class in 1948. The tender was noticeably taller as well. Mechanically they were virtual duplicates. This occurred because George Brooke, C&O's president, was pushed out by Robert R. Young in 1943, and took with him to the Virginian, the knowledge of the K-4 design and how to replicate it to fit Virginian's need. It should be noted that Virginian also built eight 2-6-6-6s that were copies of the C&O's 2-6-6-6s as part of Brooke's modernization of the Virginian.

The Richmond, Fredericksburg & Potomac also had ten 2-8-4s that were very close to the Van Sweringen standard. These locomotives were ordered during World War II and because the War Production Board insisted on using proven designs, Lima simply tacked the RF&P engines on to an order for NKP 2-8-4s that it was building. The RF&P ended up with virtual duplicates, except in outward appearance, of the NKP locomotives.

In 1947 the Pere Marquette Railway, a C&O-controlled line got its AMC 2-8-4s in the form of its N through N-2 classes. Here No. 1222 is seen new from Lima in 1941 (PM Class N-1). (C&OHS Collection, COHS 36800)

After the 1947 merger the PM 2-8-4s came to C&O's roster, but only a few of them were actually repainted before they were retired. Here C&O 2699, (ex-PM 1215) is seen at Detroit in September 1948, with rare and unusual C&O for Progress logo on the tender (only known to have been applied to two C&O locomotives, this one and a J-3). (C&OHS Collection, COHS 36801)

The five Virginian 2-8-4s were virtual copies of the NKPs. Lima photograph. (C&OHS Collection, COHS 36802)

A "cousin" of the AMC 2-8-4s was the RF&P's ten 2-8-4s, delivered from Lima in 1943, Lima photograph. (C&OHS Collection, COHS 36803)

Another cousin, perhaps once removed, was the L&N's 2-8-4's known as "Big Emmas." The L&N got 20 from Baldwin in 1942 and 22 more in 1948 at the very last of new steam. They served mainly in the Kentucky coal fields, not far from their relatives, the C&O K-4s. Lima photograph. (C&OHS Collection, COHS 36804)

The Advisory Mechanical Committee (AMC)

In November 1944 some key players in the locomotive construction game posed for Lima's official photographer commemorating completion of C&O No. 1630, first in an order for 15 more Alleghenies, bringing total to 45. A. G. Trumbull, natty in his well-fitting coat, stands on the ground fifth from left. On Trumbull's right, fourth from left, is Clyde B. Hitch of Richmond, C&O's Chief Mechanical Officer. Left of Hitch (third from left) is N. M. Trapnell, Supt. of Motive Power of Richmond. To the right of Trumbull (sixth from left) is A.H. Glass, C&O's Chief Motive Power Inspector. The AMC staff is represented by Trumbull and by Mike Donovan (third from right). Other AMC staff are in the picture, like Ed Hauer, but the identifier seemed to know only these in the front row, plus (on the end at right) Dan Ellis, Vice-President of Manufacturing for Lima since leaving his AMC post in 1943.
(C&OHS Collection, COHS 36669)

It is important to understand that almost half of all Lima Super Power production was built for four railroads, all of which were under the financial control of the Van Sweringens of Cleveland: Nickel Plate (New York, Chicago, & St. Louis), Chesapeake & Ohio, Pere Marquette, and Erie. These railroads became the strongest proponent of Lima's work, even though they also bought Super Power locomotives from other builders.

In the early part of the Twentieth Century Cleveland real estate developers O. P and M. J. Van Sweringen discovered that they needed certain properties and leases that here held by the New York, Chicago & St. Louis Railroad (known as the Nickel Plate and abbreviated NKP) to complete a rapid transit line essential to the success of their Shaker Heights development project. Since this company was controlled by the New York Central, whose president Alfred Smith (not the politician) was friendly to the Vans (as they were commonly called), they arranged to buy controlling interest in the NKP and thus entered the railroad field in 1916. The NKP was at best the poor stepchild of NYC, and needed lots of rehabilitation.

The Vans soon decided that they wanted to get into the railroad business in a bigger way, and in the mid-1920s they were able to gain control of the Erie, the Chesapeake & Ohio, the Hocking Valley, and the Pere Marquette railroads. In addition to these railroads, they purchased major interests in several other lines, but it was C&O, NKP, Erie, and PM (HV was merged into C&O in 1930) to which they paid the most attention. These companies, though they remained separate, often had the same president and officers and interlocking directorates.

The Vans used John J. Bernet as their main railroad advisor and operator. He left his position as a New York Central Vice President (at the behest of Alfred Smith) to help the Vans by becoming president of the NKP. His rehabilitation of this railroad established his credentials. He was later president of the Erie, and after that was president of C&O, NKP and PM concurrently.

Bernet was aware of the key role that appropriate motive power played in the operations and earning power of a railroad. This, of course, was near and dear to the Van Sweringens as financial manipulators of the first order.

To effect a creation of more uniform policies and plans for their group of railroads the Van Sweringen lines sent members of the managment element of their mechanical departments to a central committee, which operated out of the Cleveland headquarters with a full staff, and apparently with full authority over the mechanical operations of all the constituent railroads. This group, called the Advisory Mechanical Committee (AMC) was created in 1929.

Although records are sparse, as far as can be determined, this group had the function of overseeing the mechanical design work for the four railroads. In so doing they attempted to arrived at the best design for the work that needed to be accomplished given the characteristics of the individual railroad, but at the same time to standardize as much as possible, eliminate duplicative effort, and to ensure that the best designs were adopted by each of the lines.

Of the people who were important in the AMC's operation, foremost was Alonzo G. Trumbull who held the title "Chief Mechanical Engineer." Because of his long tenure (1929 to 1947) he had the continuity of experience to have participated in all the Super Power designs developed by the Committee for Erie, C&O, NKP and PM. Cornell educated, Trumbull was Erie's Chief Mechanical Engineer from 1922 until he moved to the AMC in 1929. He is probably the one person most responsible for the designs. D. S. Ellis, the AMC's Chief Mechanical Officer (1932-1943), and W G. Black, who was with AMC and then Vice-President of C&O, NKP, and PM all had some part, but it is apparent from research done by E. L. Huddleston that Trumbull was the "brains" of the AMC.

It appears that the AMC had the most important part in the creation of the Super Power deigns on all four railways. In addition, it also had a role in refining the design overall as used by other railroads and other builders.

The genesis of the Super Power interest on the Van Sweringen roads seems to have started in the years just before creation of the AMC when Lima, Alco, and Baldwin built the S-1,2,3, and 4 classes of huge Super Power 2-8-4s for Erie. This basic design was enlarged to create the C&O T-1 2-10-4 in 1929 (built in 1930), the first locomotive for which AMC took credit. The basic concepts were then followed in development of the famous NKP 2-8-4s, C&O's 2-8-4s, PM's 2-8-4s, and the C&O's much heralded 2-6-6-6s in subsequent years, as well as the passenger Super Power 4-8-4s and 4-6-4s for C&O.

In total between 1927 and 1949 Lima built 301 Super Power locomotives for the four Van Sweringen roads, which amounts to just under a half of its entire Super Power production, so the importance of the AMC's influence on Lima's work and vice versa should be considered in any overall evaluation of the work of either. Little original documentation survives which would show the relationships or indicate how this influence was exerted in either direction, but it can be inferred that the relationship was mutually helpful in developing and building the best possible designs within the constraints of the reciprocating steam locomotive machinery.

KANAWHA STATISTICS

Class	K-4	K-4	K-4	K-4	K-4
Road Numbers	2700-2739	2740-2749	2750-2759	2760-2784	2785-2789
Builder	ALCO	LIMA	LIMA	ALCO	ALCO
Date	1943-44	1945	1947	1947	1947
Builder's Order	S-1905	1192	1198	S-2000	S-2000
Weights: Lbs.					
On Drivers	292000	292600	293100	293100	292500
On Engine Truck	44500	47900	48500	48500	46200
On Trailing Trk	123500	128400	128080	128080	124800
Engine Total	460000	468900	469680	469680	463500
Tender	390000	393420	394100	394100	388030
Engine & Tender	850000	862320	863780	863780	851530
Boiler Pressure	245	245	245	245	245
Cylinders	26x34	26x34	26x34	26x34	26x34
Firebox	135 1/16" x 96 1/4" for all series				
Grate Area, sq. ft.	90	90	90	90	90
Total Heat. Surface	4773	4773	4714*	4714*&4773	4773
Tractive Effort	69350	69350	69350	69350	69350
T.E. Booster	14400	14000	14000	14000	14000
Total Tr. Effort	83750	83350	83350	83350	83350
Factor of Adhesion	4.21	4.21	4.23	4.23	4.21
Cyl. Horse Power	2979	2979	2979	2979	2979
Valve Gear	Baker for all series				
Superheater	Elesco Type E for all series				
Feedwater Heater	Worthington Type 5 1/2 SSA for all series				
Stoker	Std. MB	Std. HT	HT	HT	HT
Booster - Franklin	C-2-L	E	E-1	E-1	E-1
Drivers	69"	for all series			
Driving Wheel Base	18'-3"	" " "			
Length Engine	56'-4 1/2"	" " "			
Length over couplers	105'-1 7/8"	" " "			
Tender Class	21-RG	for all series			
Tender Capacity:					
Coal, tons	30	" " "			
Water, gals.	21000	" " "			

* 2750-2769 equipped with 4 circulators; all others equipped with 2 syphons.

Tender on 2749 equipped with special Buckeye Lt. Wt. trucks; all others had regular Buckeye six-wheel trucks.

This table is extracted from C&O Power, *composed by Phil Shuster, to show the comparisons among K-4 orders.* (From C&O Power, *copyright Staufer Publications, 1966)*

One place where the K-4 was liable to putting on a grand show was on the 2.67% grade of Corey Hill at Mountain Top, Kentucky on the Lexington Subdivision. Here No. 2740 is sending its exhaust to the heavens as it struggles up the grade with 1,800 tons of manifest freight in March 1952. Gene Huddleston photograph. (C&OHS Collection, COHS 1288)

CHAPTER TWO

Mechanical Specifications of the K-4 Class 2-8-4

As with any study of steam locomotives there is a need to give the principal mechanical appliances, dimensions, weights, etc. Each order of C&O K-4s is shown below with a reproduction of an official C&O mechanical diagram showing each group of locomotives within the class. Although there might be slight differences, the engines are so close to exact duplicates that C&O did not establish further sub-classes to hold the 2-8-4 wheel arrangement, but left it as a single class even though the locomotives came from different builders.

During their decade plus of operation in so wide an area of the C&O and in so many types of service, the Kanawha became an icon, which was often used in C&O advertisements, on magazine covers and even in timetables. Its appearance was, in a word, massive; yet not overpowering (as were the T-1s and H-8s). H. Stafford Bryant, who wrote the book *The Georgian Locomotive*, and spent a lifetime looking at the aesthetics of locomotives, said that if steam had lasted into the 1960s, it would have looked like C&O's latest engines, the K-4, J-3a, and L-2a classes. There is no question that the appearance of the Kanawha type was massive and compact. It simply oozed power. It is fitting that it was chosen as the one class of C&O's steam locomotives than would be preserved to the greatest degree,. A dozen still exist today. (2013).

Not only was Russell the largest and most complicated yard on the C&O, it was, in the 1950s, the largest yard owned by a single railroad in the world. Its shop was similar in nature to Clifton Forge, though smaller, and served to maintain the engines assigned to it short of the major repairs requiring that they be sent to Huntington. Here we see no less than four K-4s in the Russell shop getting work. C&O Ry. photograph.
(C&OHS Collection, CSPR 10025.493)

C&O K-4 compared with C&O K-3a Mikado

	K-3a	K-4
Weights:		
On Drivers:	274,500 lbs.	292,000 lbs.(+6.38%)
On Engine Truck:	31,000 lbs.	44,500 lbs.(+43.5 %)
On Trailing Truck:	53,500 lbs.	123,500 lbs.(+130.8%)
Engine:	350,000 lbs.	460,000 lbs.(+28.17%)
Tender:	300,000 lbs.	390,000 lbs.(+23.1%)
Engine & Tender:	659,000 lbs.	850,000 lbs.(+32.5%)
Wheels:		
Drivers	63 in.	69 in.
Engine Truck:	30 in.	44 in.
Trailing Truck:	33 in.	43 in.
Driving Wheel Base:	16 ft. 9 in.	18 ft. 3 in.
Lengths:		
Length of Engine:	49 ft. 9 in.	56 ft. 4-'/2 in.
Length over Couplers:	97 ft. 9 in.	105 ft. - 1-7/8 in.
Tender:		
Class	16-VC	21-RG
Capacity:	20 tons/16,000 gal.	30 tons/21,000 gal.
Boiler Pressure:	200 psi	245 psi
Cylinders:	28x32 in.	26x34 in.
Firebox:	121x96-1/2 in.	135-1/16x96-1/2 in.
Grate Area:	80.8 sq. ft.	90 sq. ft.
Combustion Chamber	26 in.	44 in.
Total Heating Surface:	4,459 sq. in.	4,773 sq. in.
Rated Tractive Effort:	67,700 lbs.	69,350 lbs.
Booster:	--	14,400 lbs.
Factor of Adhesion:	4.05	4.21
Horsepower (at Cylinders)	2,824	2,979
Valve Gear	Baker	Baker
Superheater:	Type A	Type E
Feedwater Heater:	Various	Worthington
Stoker:	D-1 and B	Various

The above comparison will show that the K-4 2-8-4 is larger in almost all dimensions, yet the K-3a 2-8-2 compares very well in all regards. It is easy to see why C&O delayed acquiring the 2-8-4s when it had many good, new 2-8-2s.

Comparison of 2-8-4s of the C&O, PM, NKP as well as RF&P, VGN, W&LE, and L&N

RAILROAD AND CLASS	C&O, K-4	NKP, S	PM, N	VGN, BA	R.F.&P. (no class)	L&N, M-1	L&N, M-1	W.&L.E., K-1
Numbers	2760-2789	700-714	1201-1215	505-509	571-580	1950-1963 1964-1969	1970-1991	6401-6410 6411-6415 6416-6422 6423-6432
Date Built	1947	1934	1937	1946	1943	1942.1944	1949	1937,1939 1941,1942
Builder	Alco	Alco	Lima	Lima	Lima	Baldwin	Lima	Alco
Equipped with Boosters?	Yes	No	1211-1215	No	No	Yes	Yes	No
Roller bearing?	Yes	No	No	Yes	No	Yes	Yes	Yes
Cast-steel frames with integral cyl.	Yes	No	No	Yes	Yes	Yes	Yes	No
Boiler pressure	245	245	245	245	245	265	265	245
Cylinders	26 x 34	25 x 34	26 x 34	26 x 34	25 x 34	25 x 34	25 x 34	25 x 34
Driver diameter	69	69	69	69	69	69	69	69
Tractive effort	69,350	64,100	69,350	69,350	64,100	65,290	65,290	64,135
Boiler, maximum outside diameter	98	98	98	98	98	98	98	98
Boiler, outside diameter first course	88	88	88	88	88	88	88	88
Firebox size	135 x 96	135 x 96	135 x 96	135 x 96	135 x 96	135 x 96	135 x 96	135 x 96
Grate area	90.0	90.3	90.3	90.3	90.3	90.2	90.2	90.3
Evaporative heating surface	4773	4772	4785	4773	4772	4654	4654	4718
Superheater heating surface	1932	1932	1932	1932	1932	1908	1908	2480
Driver wheelbase	18'3"	18'3"	18'3"	18'3"	18'3"	18'3"	18'3"	18'3"
Total engine wheelbase	42'0"	42'0"	42'0"	42'0"	42'0"	424"	424"	42'0"
Weight on drivers	293,100	261,100	278,100	295,600	270,900	268,200	268,200	265,500
Total weight of engine	469,680	428,900	436,500	460,400	433,200	448,100	448,100	415,000
Tender capacity	21,000 gal 30 tons	22,000 gal 22tons	22,000 gal 22 tons	25,000 gal 21 tons	22,000 gal 25 tons	22,000 gal 25 tons	22,000 gal 25 tons	22,000 gal 22 tons
Valve Gear	Baker	Baker	Baker	Baker	Baker	Walschaerts	Walschaerts	Baker

Distinctions Among Orders

	Frame	Whistle	Air Tanks	Power Reverse	
	Built Up				
2700-39 Alco	Built Up	on Steam Dome	Boiler Side	Franklin	Precision
2740-49 Lima	Cast	by Steam Dome	on Frame	Franklin	Precision
2750-59 Lima	Cast	by Stack	on Frame	Alco	
2760-84 Alco	Cast	by Stack	on Frame	Alco	
2785-89 Alco	Cast	by Stack	on Frame	Alco	

Note: *2785-2789 had welded rather than riveted boilers.*

C&O K-4 Class 2-8-4 Steam Locomotive

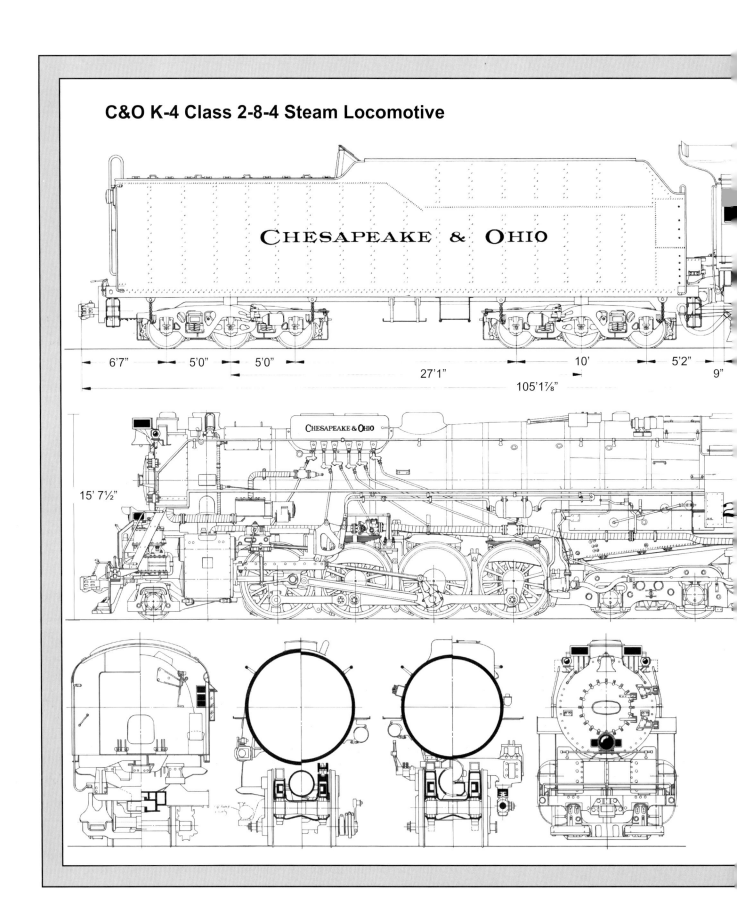

CHESAPEAKE & OHIO

6'7"   5'0"   5'0"   27'1"   10'   5'2"   9"

105'1⅞"

CHESAPEAKE & OHIO

15' 7½"

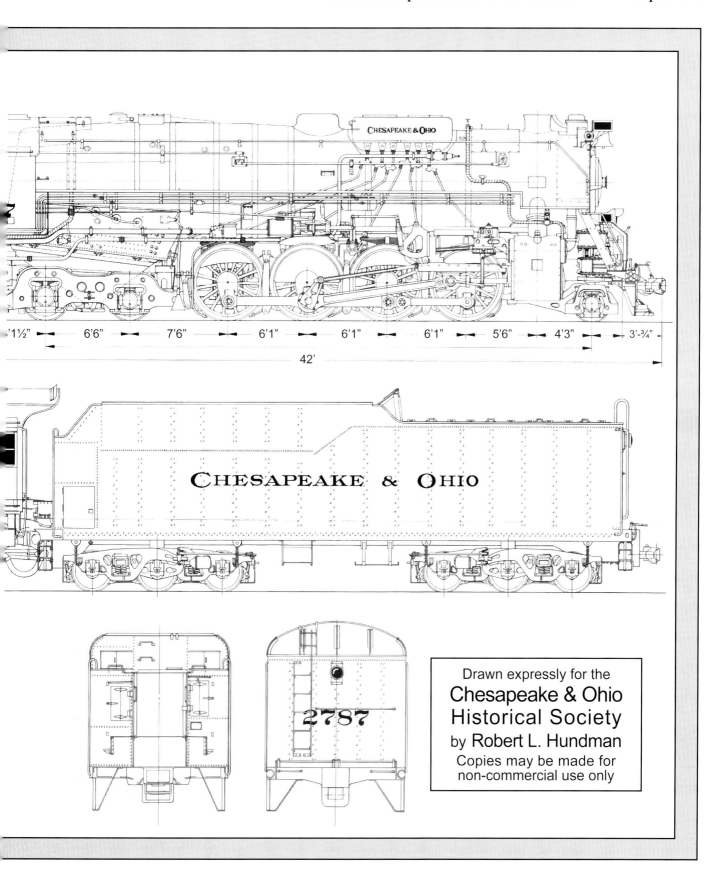

CHESAPEAKE & OHIO

'1½"   6'6"   7'6"   6'1"   6'1"   6'1"   5'6"   4'3"   3'-¾"

42'

CHESAPEAKE & OHIO

2787

Drawn expressly for the
**Chesapeake & Ohio
Historical Society**
by Robert L. Hundman
Copies may be made for
non-commercial use only

C&O Official Mechanical Diagrams for K-4 Class

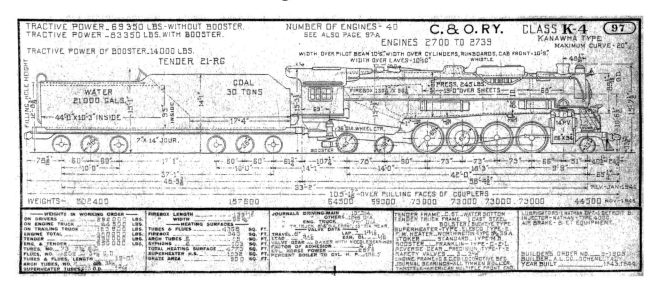

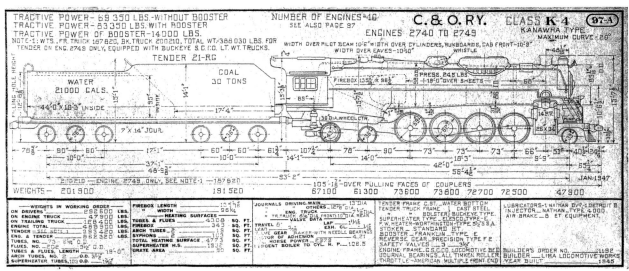

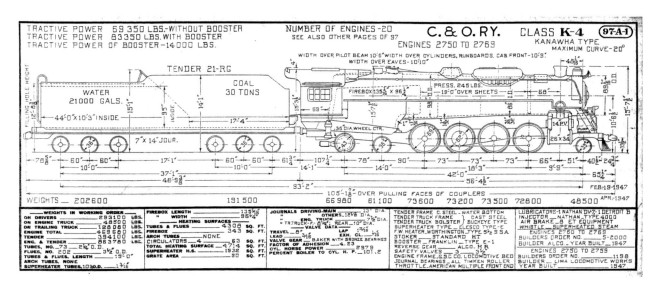

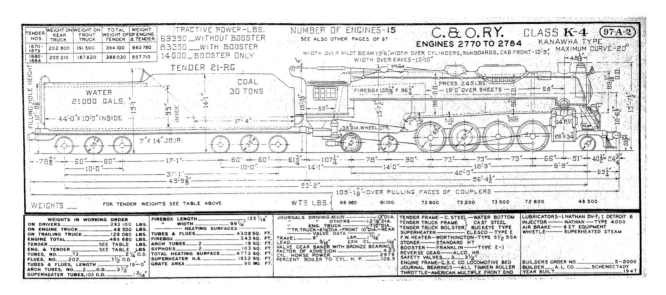

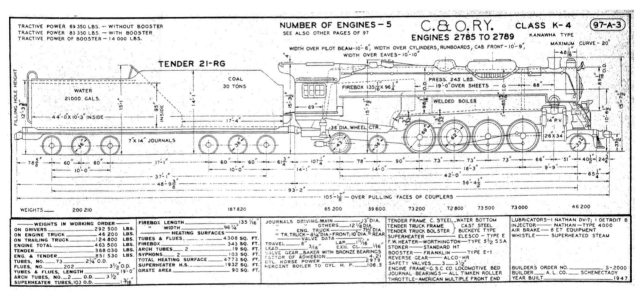

AMERICAN LOCOMOTIVE COMPANY
NEW YORK

Alco Builder Photo of No. 2730 (Represents 2700-2739)(C&OHS Collection, COHS 36653)

Lima Builder Photo of No. 2744 (Represents 2740-2749)(C&OHS Collection, CSPR 810.117)

Lima Builder Photo of No. 2754(Represents 2750-2759))(C&OHS Collection, COHS 36654)

Lima Builder Photo of No. 2786 (Represents 2785-2789) (C&OHS Collection, COHS 36656)

We do not have a builder photo of 2760-2784, so this photo of 2776 at Hinton is substituted. This particular engine is now on display at Washington Court House, Ohio. (COHS Collection, COHS 7507)

Left side of the 2730 at the builder with its tires and running boards striped in white. Though the numerals and lettering on these locomotives look white, they are imitation gold. The cab window frames are yellow.
Alco photograph. (C&OHS Collection, CSPR 810.1141)

Smokebox view of 2730 showing the clean face with oval number board, and high bell between lighted number boards that was fairly standard among the Van Sweringen lines, except the other roads had a centered headlight. The air pumps are behind the shield on the pilot beam.
Alco photograph. (C&OHS Collection, CSPR 810.115)

Rear view of 2730's tender shows just the number and capacity stenciling as well as the backup light.
Alco photograph. (C&OHS Collection, CSPR 810.116)

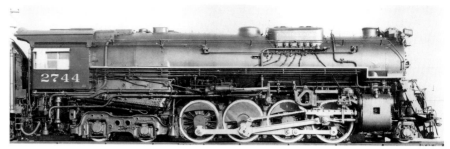

A very clean builder's view of the engine only of 2744 gives a very detailed look at the quite compact design. Note the front-end throttle reach-rod. Lima photograph. (C&OHS Collection, CSPR 810.117)

This very sharp smokebox view of 2744 represents the second order of K-4s, ten locomotives from C&O's favorite Lima. It really gives a feel for the jet black paint used on these engines. About the only difference between this batch and the first, from Alco, is the placement of the bell and the bolts beside it. (compare with Smokebox view of 2730 pg. 23). Lima photograph. (C&OHS Collection, CSPR 810.119)

The left side of 2744 is a little clearer in this builder photo that was never used for official Lima photos. Lima used the engine that they painted flat black for the photo cards and official photos. This shiny black version was supplied to the C&O for its internal use. Lima photograph. (C&OHS Collection, CSPR 810.118)

A more beautiful pose could hardly be made than this 2/3 right view of 2754, with its surroundings fully opaque out. Every element of the locomotive stands out starkly and cleanly. Lima photograph. (C&OHS Collection, COHS 36657)

Lima took many poses of 2754, this being a nice broadside left view in shiny black paint. Lima photograph. (C&OHS Collection, COHS 36655)

These close-ups of the area of the cab and firebox gives a good appreciation of the arrangement of the piping and rear truck on both sides. Lima photographs. (C&OHS Collection, CSPR 810.1212, and COHS 22933)

C&O K-4 #2754 1947 smokebox view Lima photograph. (C&OHS Collection, CSPR 810.124)

The rear view of 2754's tender. Lima photograph. (C&OHS Collection, CSPR 810.124)

Alco built the last five locomotives in 1947. No. 2786 is shown in almost left broadside at the Schenectady plant. Alco photograph. (C&OHS Collection, CSPR 810.126)

This right side view, not quite broadside, at Schenectady, shows off the last order of K-4s to good advantage and from this angle gives a good appreciation for the large tender. Alco photograph. (C&OHS Collection, CSPR 810.125)

The massive 21-RG tender is displayed in detail in this view of 2786, with even its wheel rims painted white. Considerable controversy still rages among modelers about the striping of tires and running boards. Some photos show this after the locomotives were in service, and others show no sign of it. Whether or not it was renewed at shopping is not clear. Alco photograph. (C&OHS Collection, CSPR 810.1290)

K-4 No. 2754 ready to leave Lima Locomotive Works under its own steam, to go into service at Russell. Note the Lima advertising sign attached to the running board. In this photo the brand new locomotive is really shining. (C&OHS Collection, COHS 33275)

CHAPTER THREE

Gene Huddleston on the K-4

NOTE: Eugene L. Huddleston was one of the best, and also best known, photographers who covered the last years of steam on the C&O. Son of a C&O conductor out of Russell, Kentucky, Gene became actively interested in taking photos of locomotives in his middle 'teens, and took his first photos in 1947. He got a good camera and became connected with Rail Photo Service, which supplied film to photographers all over the country. The RPS photographers then sent in the negatives in exchange for 5x7 prints. This was a good way for Gene and others to fund their hobby. Over the years Gene became a college professor and eventually taught at Michigan State University in East Lansing. He took slides starting about 1957 and continued until his death in 2010. Gene took many C&O photos in areas that other photographers never ventured, including the coal branches of West Virginia and Kentucky. He was also a superb researcher and among the most knowledgeable about steam power. In 2005 he authored the book *Chesapeake & Ohio Super Power Steam Locomotives*, published by the C&O Historical Society, the last of his many books on railroads and other subjects. The following is from this book's chapter on the K-4s, and gives a unique perspective of someone who not only studied these locomotives, but also experienced and photographed many of them for almost a decade.

A heavy coal train is headed west on the Cincinnati Division at Greenup, Kentucky, with K-4 No. 2713 for power in June 1951. Fresh ballast has been added to the siding in the foreground. Gene Huddleston photograph.
(C&OHS Collection, COHS 1309)

2708 has in charge fast manifest freight train "Advance No. 92" just leaving Russell, Ky. for the eastern cities in June 1950. Gene Huddleston photograph. (C&OHS Collection, COHS 1100)

It was mostly business as usual when in 1943 and into 1944 the first 30 of what would eventually be 90 2-8-4s showed up at the busy freight terminal at Russell, Kentucky. They came from the Alco plant at Schenectady, New York. War impacted on their construction to the extent of requiring a steel bell (going "clank, clank") instead of the customary brass bell, and shortages led to other substitutions for copper and copper alloys. After the War, "real" bells were retrofitted. The last 10 of the first order of 40, supplied with steam, heat, air communications lines and automatic train controls, went into service at Clifton Forge, Virginia, hauling passenger trains and time freights over the Mountain Subdivision. The men at Russell (I don't know about Clifton Forge) called them "Big Mikes." Officially they were classed by C&O Motive Power Department as class K-4, the "K" slot reserved for all Mikados (but they were not really Mikados) and the "4" for the fourth variation in design among orders for new Mikados and their Super Power cousins.

C&O Mechanical Department officials in Richmond, Virginia knew they could trust the designs of the Advisory Mechanical Committee, for by 1943 the road had already been rewarded by superb performances of the big Texas type 2-10-4s of 1930, the J-3 4-8-4s of 1935, the Allegheny 2-6-6-6s of 1941, and the class L-2 4-6-4s of 1942 - all AMC designs. Such trust was necessary because of the geographical separation of the AMC headquarters in Cleveland from the C&O's in Richmond.

In 1934, the AMC down scaled the very successful 2-10-4 to a 2-8-4 with 70% of the T-1's tractive effort and weight. American Locomotive Company (Alco) made the low bid and constructed the first 15 of an eventual order of 80 Nickel Plate Berkshires Engines 715-779 would all come from Lima Locomotive Works. The AMC even made parts of the 2-10-4 interchangeable with the 2-8-4. The reason nine years elapsed before the AMC considered the 2-8-4 design for C&O was that C&O had in service throughout the Depression 150 heavy Mikados classed as K-2 and K-3. The K-3s hauled 160 loaded coal cars down the James River line from the base of the Alleghenies to Richmond and came back, unassisted, with that many empties.

The NKP moved along in the 1920's and early 1930's with light Mikados, mainly because its manifest freight trains were lighter in tonnage than C&O's solid coal trains. NKP's Mikados, which were built in the early Twenties, were essentially the standardized USRA light Mikado type, getting a heft in starting power with trailer boosters. They could move tonnage along but at "drag era" speeds. The problem was the NKP ran parallel with the main line of New York Central. While the NYC thought it could haul its trains at "drag era" speeds, NKP knew that to keep the competitive edge which it did under capable presidents like Bernet and Davin later it needed to haul freight faster than its huge, but bumbling, neighbor. Here, the AMC came to the rescue in its first design job since the T-1 of 1930. It knew clearances would not permit an engine as big as the T-1. Also, the tonnage and grade requirements were less than with the T-1s. It scaled down the T-1, and kept the same general appearance, especially the "face" of the locomotive, for the NKP Berkshires.

The K-4s were the standard power for almost all freights on the Kanawha Subdivision between Handley, W. Va. and Russell, Ky. They also powered coal trains up and down two of the major coal districts joining with the Kanawha Subdivision, the Coal River and Logan districts. Here 2725 and 2737 share space at the St. Albans coaling station and terminal area with G-9 2-8-0 No. 1025. The Coal River Subdivision joined the mainline at this point. Gene Huddleston photograph. (C&OHS Collection, COHS 1816)

As soon as it became apparent what a "winner" NKP had in the AMC-designed 2-8-4s, the PM, along with the C&O, ordered two of the NKP design. One important change, however, was 26-inch cylinder bores instead of 25 inch for all NKP's. (A proportional on drivers kept adhesion on both engines the same.) Front end styling on both models was almost identical, with the form of the pilot the only significant difference until NKP alone added Mars oscillating headlights above the standard headlights. All NKP and most PM 2-8-4s had "bar" frames instead of solid cast frames and lacked roller bearings - economy moves probably.

Recounting how the Pere Marquette got its first Super Power Berkshires from the AMC is as good a place as any to deal with the placement of the steam dome on the boiler top on the NKP S class the PM N class and the C&O K class of 2-8-4s. It is as much an aesthetic as a practical consideration. The Chief Mechanical Engineer of the AMC, Alonzo Trumbull, placed the steam dome near the front of the boiler on the huge 2-10-4 that he designed for the C&O in 1930. Presumably this made for more space in the boiler for generating steam, for the big pipe (called the "dry pipe") leading from the dome to the throttle

valves could be made shorter than if it ran from a dome located farther back on the boiler. Yet placing the dome well forward on a conical-shaped boiler meant that to insure the dry pipe would remain free of foaming water overflowing into it. The dome would have to be built up higher than it would if the dome were placed near the highest point of the conical boiler. That was a point just forward of the end of the combustion chamber. Trumbull evidently discovered, with the T-1, there were no overflow problems with the dome placed well forward, so he carried the proportional placement and size over into the design of the NKP 2-8-4s. As it turned out, all 80 NKP 2-8-4s adhered to this placement. Just three years after designing the NKP 2-8-4s, Trumbull copied the same location and same dimensions for the first order of Pere Marquette 2-8-4s. Ditto for the second PM order in 1941. However, in 1944 PM's 1228-1239 engines featured the steam dome just forward of the section of the boiler, marking its maximum outside diameter of 98 inches. The year 1942 seemed to be the pivotal year in this design dilemma. For in 1942, C&O's second order of 4-8-4s from the AMC (unlike the first in 1936) had the steam dome behind the sand box, as did C&O's L-2 class Hudsons from

These two photos show a virtually unknown pusher operation that occurred for a few years in the early 1950s, when heavy trains out of Handley, the eastern terminal of the Kanawha Subdivision, used a pair of K-4s to Hinton. The usual practice at the time was to assign a single 2-6-6-6 H-8 from Handley east (H-8s never regularly went west of Handley on the Kanawha SD). Here No. 2770 is the road engine on this eastbound coal drag in August 1955, in the last full year of steam, while the second photo shows 2749 on the rear of the train. The train is passing the wooden water tank at Mt. Carbon, W. Va. The weedy branch line in the foreground in the Powellton Subdivision. Gene Huddleston photograph. (C&OHS Collection, COHS 1184, 1185)

K-4 No. 2778 is taking an empty coal train down the line to Peach Creek yard at Logan, where the cars will be dispersed to the scores of mines on this, one of the most productive of C&O branch lines. Note that a refrigerator car has been tacked on at the head of the train. This was often done for fast freight headed for the coal fields where regular local freights and through trains were not always available for such shipments. Placing it behind the engine allowed the hoppers to be dropped and then the refrigerator car moved on up to the terminal for placement on the consignee's track. Gene Huddleston photograph. (C&OHS Collection, COHS 1156)

Baldwin and C&O's 2-8-4s which started arriving on the property in 1943.

By December 7, 1941, the C&O had received the first of its magnificent new Allegheny articulateds, plus new eight-wheel switchers, two new 4-8-4s and seven new 4-6-4s - all Super Power except the switchers. The 150 heavy Mikes still were rugged performers, but they were not Super Power, and C&O wanted engines that were less in need of maintenance than the older engines with their "built up" frames and solid bearings. The new C&O engines would have roller bearings on all engine axles and solid engine beds with cylinders in one big casting. In later orders for the C&O 2-8-4s, the main air reservoir was made part of this casting, set in the frame above the two rear driving axles.

Rated starting tractive effort of the C&O 2-8-4s was 69,350 lbs. This is 5,250 lbs. more than NKP's 2-8-4s, mainly because of increased weight on drivers of the C&O (and Pere Marquette) engines, plus the inch larger cylinder bore. All ninety C&O 2-8-4s, plus 10 of the 39 PM 2-8-4s were equipped with booster engines on the rear axle of the trailing truck, which added tractive power at starting or near

stalling speed when moving. Because all C&O Super Power locomotives had boosters (with exception of the 2-6-6-6, which nevertheless had provision for one) one gets curious about them. Trailing trucks had adhesive weight that made it practical unlike tender axles with varying adhesive weights for power to be supplied to the wheels.

Other roads using the Van Sweringen design may have put boosters on their 2-8-4s, depending largely on topography and tonnage. The Virginian Railway, the Wheeling and Lake Erie, and the Richmond, Fredericksburg, and Potomac did not adopt them; all 42 of the Louisville and Nashville's 2-8-4s, nicknamed "Big Emmas," did. Both the Virginian and L&N hauled long coal trains, but the Virginian had bigger engines than 2-8-4s (which were intended for manifests) to haul its coal - the eight 2-6-6-6s of 1945. The L&N hauled long coal trains, mostly out of eastern Kentucky, to northern markets: it also had more severe gradients for its northbound coal than the Virginian had for its eastbound coal. Unlike the Virginian, the L&N had no bigger engines than the M-1 2-8-4s (of 1942, 1944, and 1949). These engines put on a real show hauling coal trains from the level of the Kentucky River to the Bluegrass Plateau near

K-4 No. 2735 is on fast freight No. 92 leaving Russell in July 1947 in the days when box cars carried the nation's merchandise. Gene Huddleston photograph. (C&OHS Collection, COHS 1472)

Winchester. At Ford, on the river, an M-1 pusher would wait for double headed M-1s from Corbin, each with about 8,500 tons of coal. The pusher assisted the doubleheader up steep Two Mile Creek toward Patio Tower, getting down to seven m.p.h.. with all boosters cut in on the 1.07% grade, for nine miles.

Because the booster was applied to the trailing axle of the trailing truck, the increased tractive effort it provided had little effect on the factor of adhesion, which normally went down as the tractive effort went up relative to the weight on drivers. Boosters did not "slip" easily because they made use of "wasted" dead weight that had no effect on the weight on drivers. Nevertheless, boosters could slip, as evidenced by the fact that one of the six pipes leading downward (on each side) from the K-4's huge sand box fed the front of the powered trailer wheels. The stream of sand dropped on the track just ahead of the powered wheel and definitely improved traction.

On the C&O 2-8-4s, the booster, which cut out at 15 mph, added 14,000 lbs to the starting tractive effort of 69,350 lbs. Of course, if the booster was not cut in, it could not add that boost of power. That's why on some roads prevailing opinion was

that boosters were extraneous. S. Kip Farrington, Jr., sportsman, railfan, and author, was an anti-booster man: "The booster never made much impression on me. It was just one more extravagance to get out of order and was so many times never 'cut in.' One would in fact, be amazed at what little usage boosters received..." Whether C&O locomotive engineers obeyed instructions is not known nevertheless, C&O prescribed their use in every case where the locomotive was accelerating from a stop to road speed, or had fallen below a certain speed and in danger of stalling, despite a wide-open throttle. The two-cylindered reciprocating engines, "splash" lubricated, had only forward motion. When "cut in" by the engineer (through compressed air),their rapid exhaust from a slot in front of the stack added to the impression of power produced.

One place to look for solid data on booster usage is in reports of locomotive performance from data gathered on C&O's dynamometer car, DM-1. Luckily one such report has been preserved. C&O's "Engineer of Tests," issuing it in August 1951, recommended an increase in tonnage in both directions following extensive testing of C&O's class K-4 2-8-4s over the scenic and (constructed in the 1850s) across the

C&O K-4 #2755 with empty hopper drag stopping for water at Sproul, W.Va. on the Coal River Subdivison in July 1949 photo by Gene Huddleston. (C&OHS Collection, COHS 1810)

The terminal at Handley was a busy place as it hosted trains arriving and parting on the Kanawha Subdivision west and the New River Subdivision east. Here 2728 is bringing in a train from the west while 2704 is coupled on a coal train that looks ready to depart westbound. The large structure in the distance on the left is the Handley lock and dam on the Kanawha River. Gene Huddleston photograph. (C&OHS Collection, COHS 1300)

The through truss Guyandot River bridge in the eastern suburbs of Huntington is the scene as 2704 takes No. 92 east while gathering speed in November 1951. Gene Huddleston photograph. (C&OHS Collection, COHS 2044)

Alleghanies and Blue Ridge, a line aptly named the Mountain Subdivision. The main finding of the report stated, "Dynamometer car tests indicate that the present straight tonnage rating can be increased ... with no danger of stalling providing full use is made of the booster." "Full use" of course meant starting and cutting in when speed falls under 13.5 mph. The real test of the K-4's mettle was when stops were deliberately made on the ruling grade in each direction "with tonnage exceeding the recommended." Lowest permissible speed on westbound ruling grade was 15 mph and on the eastbound 12.5 mph. To attain the summit of momentum grades such as Longdale Hill, speed could fall to 8 mph. One can be sure that the booster was used in every situation for which it was intended. The K-4s were picked randomly from the Clifton Forge pool of 2-8-4s; however, engines in the 2760 series predominated because they were equipped with Automatic Train Control devices, in

use over the Mountain Subdivision. On board for all runs were the "Division Trainmaster and the Road Foreman [of engines]."

After the war, freight tonnage continued to be handled quite well without need of an articulated and without assistance from a "helper" engine.) Figures from 2768's run up the grade, from the rolling Piedmont west of Charlottesville to the summit at Blue Ridge Tunnel, show that on August 8, 1951, 2768 commanded 50 cars, or 1623 tons. The train stopped and started again without difficulty on the steepest part of the grade (because of curvature) just east of Little Rock Tunnel. Here the ascent of the Blue Ridge was up a nine mile grade that averaged 1.40%. This tonnage being 123 tons above the rating for a K-4 westbound, the tonnage rating was subsequently increased to 1600 tons. On the eastbound run the longest sustained pull was between Augusta Springs

Gene has captured a nice going way shot that showcases the giant 21-RG tender of No. 2776 as it approaches Russell with a coal drag from Peach Creek and the Logan fields in April 1954.   By this date about 70% of the C&O was dieselized, with the New River, Kanawha, Logan, and Coal River lines the last strongholds of steam locomotives, principal among them the K-4s. Gene Huddleston photograph. (C&OHS Collection, COHS 2048)

and North Mountain station at the summit of Great North Mountain, which averaged 1.50%. On August 2, 1951, No. 2763 stopped with 27 cars, 1875 tons, two miles east of Augusta Springs, and started - the booster cut in, of course - with "no difficulty." Because of this, the previous rating was increased from 1750 tons to 1780 tons. One wonders why only a 30-ton increase here and why the tests had not been done years before! (It would only be a couple of years before the Mountain Sub was completely dieselized.)

Other than for piston displacement, principal dimensions for the 2-8-4s of the three Van Sweringen roads were generally the same. However, the C&O engines, from front coupler to end of cab, were slightly longer than the PM and NKP 2-8-4s. The difference resulted from roomier cabs. "Railway Age" observed in its write-up of the C&O 2-8-4s that the company had consulted officials of the Brotherhoods - presumably the B of LE and the BLF&E - on cab size. This consultation resulted in lengthening the cab. All ninety C&O K-4s had cabs 95 1/8 inches long, whereas the Nickel Plate and Pere Marquette 2-8-4s were 88 3/4 inches long. Three men were expected to ride in some comfort in the cab: engineer, fireman, and head brakeman.

Because the Great Depression was history and world warfare produced a booming economy, the

C&O in 1943 could afford the AMC's recommendation that all engine axles be supplied with roller bearings. Previous to this, even C&O's AMC designed passenger locomotives did not have roller bearings. Although carriage maker Henry Timken invented the tapered roller bearing in 1898, it took a long time for the bearings to come to the railroad industry. Even in the booming 1920's Timken (of Canton, Ohio) could not motivate railroads to buy new locomotives with driving axles cradled in roller bearings. Perhaps railroads thought them too expensive, considering that the driving boxes in which the axles rode were subject to so much stress that necessary maintenance on the boxes overrode the bearings' advantages of not requiring frequent maintenance.

By 1943, the AMC wanted the new "Van Sweringen" Berkshires to be among the best equipped of modern power, so cast steel frames (with attachments and cylinders cast integrally), roller bearings, boosters, and air after-coolers guaranteed their modernity. Also, by 1943 Westinghouse Air Brake Company had designed air after-cooler units that were wholly self-contained. This meant that the C&O 2-8-4 front end would have a different look than the NKP and PM engines, which were not equipped with after-coolers. Ventilating grids cooled the air compressed by two cross compound compressors,

K-4 2710 is hauling Manifest "CD-93" westward on the Cincinnati Division at Wurtland, Kentucky, just west of the Russell yard in the summer of 1953. Gene Huddleston photograph. (C&OHS Collection, COHS 1214)

The K-4s were certainly at home on passenger trains, the entire class being equipped with steam and communication lines. They were often and regularly used until the number of mainline trains was cut in October 1948 concurrent with the arrival of new passenger power. No. 2769 is seen here powering No. 5, the westbound Sportsman, out of Clifton Forge in April 1948, with a solid heavyweight train. Gene Huddleston photograph.
(C&OHS Collection, COHS 1172)

mounted on either side of the unit. Compressing air generated a great deal of heat (and moisture) in the process. The need for protecting the cooling unit from the elements resulted in the C&O 2-8-4s having a unique and well-balanced front end. On the front end of the K-4 the purity of the smokebox front was preserved by keeping the headlight and classification lights off it, and the positioning of the headlight midway between coupler and bell was a master touch. A single functional shield protecting air after-cooler unit and twin air pumps gave further distinction to the design, for while it left the face of the smokebox completely uncovered, it seemed to divide the front end into three equal and complementary parts: the pilot, the shield (and headlight), and smokebox door. The tripartite harmony was also preserved in the three part pilot - a deflector placed between twin footboards, all three equally proportioned - as well as in the bell placed between two large illuminated number plates (the K-4 being the first new engines on C&O factory equipped with the plates)."

Perhaps the greatest moment of glory for a K-4 on the hill-bound Lexington Division was in 1948; two K-4s - with 2787 in the lead - hauled the 17-car campaign train of President Harry S. Truman from Lexington, Ky. to Ashland, Ky. and beyond. What an impressive sight was this train of heavyweight coaches and Pullmans, headed by the two big Kanawhas and trailed by the huge, armored "Ferdinand Magellan," with its open platform from which the President spoke. A doubleheader was run because in climbing the 2.67% of Corey Hill a pusher could not be placed behind the president's car. In addition to "Varnish" on the scenic Lexington Division, K-4s on the main line took long trains of "day coaches," after World War II ended, on weekend baseball excursions from Charleston, West Virginia, picking up along the way, to Cincinnati. The ease of transportation to Cincinnati and the fact that Crosley Field was in easy walking distance from the Union Station made for a great gathering of baseball fans. During both World War II and the Korean War the

K-4's handled many military movements, because of C&O's access to the string of bases in northern Virginia and naval facilities at Hampton Roads. Troop, hospital, and prisoner-of-war trains were given whatever power was available, and K-4s had a record of dependability. Altogether, about 70 of the 90 K-4s were equipped with steam heat lines and air communication lines needed to haul passenger trains.

Another interesting passenger movement handled by K-4s is recalled by Joe Slanser of Marion, Ohio. The all-important football rivalry between Ohio State and the University of Michigan merited its own special train every fall (last game of season for both) between Columbus and Ann Arbor. Mr. Slanser recalls, back in 1947 or 1948, riding it to Ann Arbor, with a K-4 on the head end. While clickedy-clacking

across the glacial outwash plains of northern Ohio, he asked the conductor how fast they were going, and the conductor obligingly took out his pocket Ingersoll and timed their passage by a couple of mile posts at 70 mph. The employee timetable in his possession had a chart for converting elapsed time per mile into speed. (As an aside, that speed should not be too surprising since it was a rule of thumb that a steam locomotive could cruise at a speed equal to the diameter of its driver height in inches - 69 inches for the class K-4.)

K-4 No. 2740 en route from either Handley or Russell with a train of empties, is about to pass the 200-ton wooden coaling station at Sproul in 1948. This is the only really good, clear photo we have of this classic structure. Gene Huddleston photograph. (C&OHS Collection, COHS 33077)

CHAPTER FOUR

K-4s in Operation 1944-1956

This chapter consists of photos showing the K-4 Kanawha 2-8-4s in operation all across the C&O system. The photos are arranged geographically east-to-west to illustrate the diversity of operations and areas in which these versatile locomotives were used during the dozen years that they plied C&O rails. Included is a map showing the areas where the K-4s were used. However, it should be noted that based on memories, operational records, and photographic evidence, the K-4s were used in some regions much more heavily than in others. For example, the regions east of Hinton had much fewer of these locomotives in regular service than the areas west of there. According to Gene Huddleston, writing in the book *The Van Sweringen Berkshires* (NJ International, 1986) they were used as the "principal road freight locomotive" on certain lines. The following table (see page 44) is Gene's compilation.

K-4 No. 2735 is on fast freight No. 92 leaving Russell in July 1947 in the days when box cars carried the nation's merchandise. Gene Huddleston photograph. (C&OHS Collection, COHS 1472)

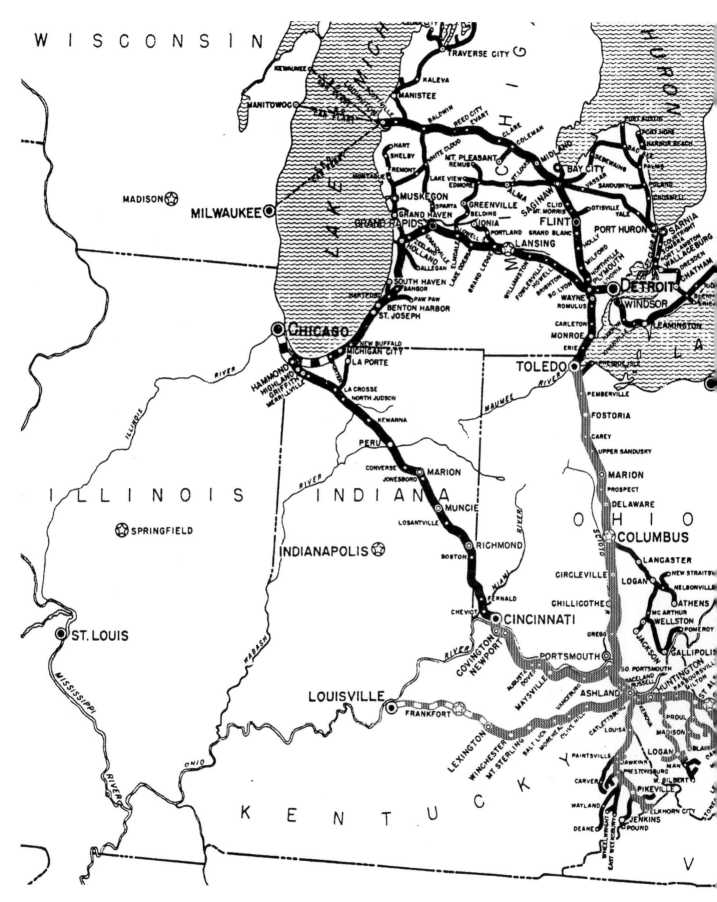

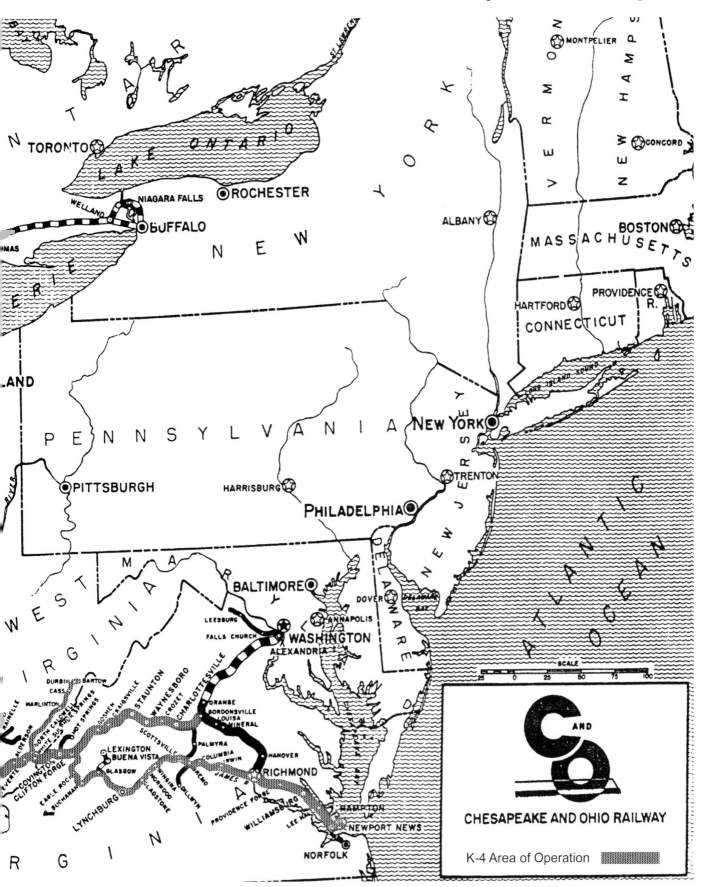

CHESAPEAKE AND OHIO RAILWAY

K-4 Area of Operation

From	To	Distance	Sub-division
Cincinnati (Stevens Yd., KY.)	Russell, Ky.	227	Cincinnati
Russell, Ky.	Martin, Ky.	100	Big Sandy
Russell, Ky.	Shelby, Ky.	124	Big Sandy
Russell, Ky.	Elkhorn City, Ky.	140	Big Sandy
Russell, Ky.	Lexington, Ky.	128	Lexington
Russell, Ky.	Handley, W. Va.	94	Kanawha
Russell, Ky.	Logan, W. Va.	93	Kanawha and Logan
Russell, Ky.	Danville, W. Va.	94	Kanawha and Coal River
Russell, Ky.	Whitesville, W. Va.	107	Kanawha and Big Coal
Russell, Ky.	Cane Fork, W. Va.	96	Kanawha and Cabin Creek
Clifton Forge, Va.	Charlottesville, Va.	95	Mountain

However, we do find K-4s in use in other areas with some consistency, but not nearly as the principal freight locomotive class:

- On the Peninsula Subdivision they had occasional use on coal trains.

- On the James River Subdivision between Clifton Forge-Gladstone they were occasionally used on coal trains in the last years of steam and on the Rivanna Subdivision between Gladstone-Richmond.

- On the Mountain Subdivision they were on fast freights and passenger trains.

- Their use on the Alleghany Subdivision was occasionally as pushers westbound Clifton Forge-Alleghany, and on local freights or manifest freights when tonnage allowed and/or they needed to be moved westward toward Huntington for shop cycles or reassignment, often used on passenger trains until late 1948.

- They were used occasionally on the Greenbrier Subdivision for the local freights during the waning years of steam, supplanting 2-6-6-2s.

- On the New River Subdivision they saw occasional use on passenger trains and on through freights, but this was rare. In passenger service until late 1948.

- On the Northern Subdivision K-4s can be seen on coal trains instead of T-1s or H-8s, but only rarely. They were apparently regularly used only on manifest freights.

- They seldom seem to have ventured north (west by railroad direction) but do appear in a few photos at the Detroit terminal. Our inference here is that they got there on passenger trains or possibly manifest freights.

- They do not seem to have been used on the Chicago Division, nor on coal branches other than Coal River, Logan and Big Sandy, for operational considerations such as weight and clearances.

The K-4s were suited for a variety of work and were actually a modern replacement for the Mikados. The work that K-2, 3 and 3a types were doing quickly became the K-4's work, yet because they came during the height of the World War II and post-war traffic boom, there was still plenty of work for the older Mikados. However, in the post-war era when the choice for assignment was between available Mikados or Kanawhas, the 2-8-4s usually got the work. After all, during their operational life they were "new" locomotives. And, they had all the latest appliances and were more powerful and better steamers overall.

As the end of steam loomed it was the Mikados that were retired and the K-4s kept going to the very end, so if you see a photo in the last years of steam in the 1950s you are far more likely to see a K-4, H-4,5,6 or an H-8 than any other locomotive classes.

K-4 No. 2716 (now on display at the Kentucky Railroad Museum, New Haven, Ky.) starts a train west out of Newport News yard with some box cars up front, followed by a long string of hoppers about 1950 as 0-8-0 No. 251 switches at left. K-4s were not the regular power on the Peninsula Subdivision. (C&OHS Collection, COHS 36658)

No. 2728 is in charge of a coal train at Williamsburg in November 1947. It can be inferred that the K-4s were the heaviest power available for coal drags on the Peninsula in the late 1940s. It wasn't until 1950 that the T-1s and H-8s were transferred here, pulled dead over the Richmond viaduct, and put into rotating Richmond-Newport News coal train service. C. N. Lippencott photograph. (C&OHS Collection, COHS 1713)

The C&O K-4 Class 2-8-4 Steam Locomotive   45

Lots of steam frames this moody photo of K-4 No. 2762 at the Charlottesville engine terminal in February 1948. Judson Smith photograph. (C&OHS Collection, COHS 2493)

Looking sharp as any passenger locomotive, 2763 powers all-heavyweight No. 5, the Sportsman out of Charlottesville at Farmington, Va., in about 1948. Bruce Fales photograph. (C&OHS Collection, COHS 2763)

No. 2769 is about to enter Little Rock Tunnel on the Blue Ridge grade on August 20, 1951 with a fast freight in tow. H. Reid photograph. (C&OHS Collection, COHS 36660)

At the Portal of the new Blue Ridge Tunnel (opened 1942), No. 2761 has No. 92, one of the four hot manifests on the Mountain Subdivision, July 15, 1949. J. I. Kelly photograph. (C&OHS Collection, COHS 36661)

An often used photo, but none better to illustrate this material than K-4s 2763 and 2761 with what is probably No. 5, The Sportsman, *charging west from Staunton at Swope, Va. in 1949. C&O Ry. Photograph. (C&OHS Collection, CSPR 2356)*

K-4 No. 2730 and another locomotive move west through the Clifton Forge yard complex at the passenger station area (Smith Creek yard office in background left), in July 1946. C&O Ry. photograph. (C&OHS Collection, CSPR 640)

Ready to take a passenger train east, 2764 sits in front of the Clifton Forge depot/YMCA and division office building at Clifton Forge in the fall of 1950. B. F. Cutler Photograph. (C&OHS Collection, COHS 1329)

K-4 No. 2762 double heads with J-3 Greenbrier No. 606 on Train No. 4, The Sportsman, about to leave Clifton Forge in the winter of 1948. (C&OHS Collection, COHS 1817)

A rare set of photos shows K-4 No. 2762 pushing a manifest freight train westbound at Alleghany, Va. In September 1950. Manifests usually rated an H-8 out of Clifton Forge and required no pusher to Alleghany, but on this date a pusher was required for some reason, either the road power was a K-4 also or the train was too heavy. We know of this occurring on occasion, but rarely. B. F. Cutler photographs. (C&OHS Collection, COHS 1850 and COHS 36662)

A ten-car No. 47, The Sportsman, is powered by K-4 2769 as it passes WS Cabin, just west of White Sulphur Springs in July 1947. From 1943 until late 1948 many C&O mainline trains operated in two sections. No. 47 was followed by No. 5 by an hour and 10 minutes. (No. 5 operated Washington-Cincinnati, whereas No. 47 ran Phoebus-Detroit. In this era where there was no combination of sections Charlottesville-Ashland.) J. I. Kelly photograph.
(C&OHS Collection, COHS 348)

No. 2772 rests at the Ronceverte engine terminal May 24, 1953 waiting assignment to a freight on the Greenbrier Branch to Durbin. The K-4s replaced 2-6-6-2s ad K-2, or K-3s on the Greenbrier branch in the early 1950s.
(C&OHS Collection, COHS 36663)

K-4 2729 has mail and passenger train westbound at Hawks Nest, W. Va. in about 1947. After arrival of J-3a and L-2a passenger power and the elimination of second sections in 1948, K-4s were taken off of their passenger duties except as needed for specials, etc. C&O Ry. photograph. (C&OHS Collection, CSPR 1036)

Hauling an eastbound manifest freight at MacDougal (near Hawks Nest) No. 2706 is about to take the South Main Line in the 1947 photo. C&O Ry. photograph. (C&OHS Collection, CSPR 1017)

Another K-4, 2745 powers a westbound manifest crossing the Hawks Nest Bridge at MacDougle in 1947. The day that the C&O photographer was at this spot, K-4s had a lot of the action. C&O Ry. photograph. (C&OHS Collection, CSPR 1011)

This wonderful action photo shows 2780 rolling an empty train west as an auto speeds along Kanawha Boulevard in Charleston in June 1951. W. G. Francher photograph. (C&OHS Collection, COHS 1394)

At the Charleston depot 2789 the last of the K-4s bring in the American Friendship Train in the winter of 1949. This was a special train of food stuffs collected by donation that was sent to Newport News and forwarded to Europe for post-war relief. T. L. Wise photograph. (C&OHS Collection, COHS 10821)

An operational problem n the Kanawha Subdivision was the grade westbound out of St. Albans, which required pushers for coal trains. Here K-4 2788 has his train in hand at Teays in May 1949. The pusher, out of sight is a 2-6-6-2. Gene Huddleston photograph. (C&OHS Collection, COHS 1197)

His rare overhead photo shows 2748 with a coal train (with some miscellaneous freight up front) at Culloden, W. Va. in the fall of 1953. C&O Ry. photograph. (C&OHS Collection, CSPR 3183)

A coal train from Logan is arriving at the western edge of Huntington in the summer of 1955, during the last full year of steam on the C&O. B. J. Kern photograph. (C&OHS Collection, COHS 2744)

Near Huntington in 1954, No. 2717 has an empty train in tow. Note the long cantilever signal tower so familiar along C&O line and the full 3-track signal bridge in the distant background. The blast plates on the signal tower are prominent from this angle. C&O Ry. photograph. (C&OHS Collection, CSPR 10025.498)

The old and the new: K-4 2707 with empty hoppers at left and Alco RS-2 diesel No. 5587 at Huntington yard June 1953. Gene Huddleston photograph. (C&OHS Collection, COHS 7507)

Just west of Huntington, K-4 2787 has a hopper train with a few box cars at Kenova, where the N&W's main line passes over the C&O (see station platform in far distance) and B&O's Ohio River Division joined C&O. Gene Huddleston photograph. (C&OHS Collection, COHS 1004)

A classic scene, with 2747 at speed with a coal train passing two rows of loaded hoppers on the main line near Huntington in 1953. C&O Ry. photograph. (C&OHS Collection, CSPR 3182)

A great photo taken by C&O's publicity department, shows 2747 with fast freight No. 92 passing over the Big Sandy bridge between Catlettsburg, Ky. and Kenova, W. Va. in September 1946. The bridge's restrictions were a problem for C&O's T-1s until the bridge was strengthened in 1948, allowing the monster 2-10-4s to operate east of Russell. C&O Ry. photograph. (C&OHS Collection, CSPR 57.174)

The K-4s were much used in C&O's publicity photographs and advertising. Here in 1944, the official photographer shows 2719 and its train near the large Armco blast furnace at Ashland, Ky., at one time C&O's largest single customer. C&O Ry. photograph. (C&OHS Collection, CSPR 202)

Night at Ashland station was a busy affair a trains came and went to and from Cincinnati, Louisville, Washington, and Detroit. It was here that the sections we combined and separated. No. 2775 is going about its passenger business in December 1948. C&O Ry. photograph. (C&OHS Collection, CSPR 2227)

No. 2712 is seen here moving a westbound coal train near BS Cabin, Big Sandy Junction, in Catlettsburg, Kentucky in July 1945, with coal off the Big Sandy branches. K-4s were commonly used to bring coal from Big Sandy marshalling yards. The full signal bridge in the background was characteristic of the multiple track line through Catlettsburg. (C&O Ry. Photo, C&OHS Collection, CSPR 57.073).

The modeler wanting to weather a locomotive could look at 2713 at Russell, taken in May 1953, its back 1/3rd white with sand dusting. (C&OHS Collection, COHS 36666)

This beautiful photo epitomizes the K-4 in action as it hauls general freight and hoppers east from Russell in December 1951, the Ohio River barely visible through the trees at right, and the white steam exhaust telling all the world that steam was still working on the C&O. Gene Huddleston photograph. (C&OHS Collection, COHS 1192)

Coal trains headed to the mainline from the Danville, W. Va. marshalling yard were usually handled by K-4s in their era. Here, in June 1950, a K-4 is seen at the Danville engine terminal waiting to take a train of loads to either Handley or Russell. Gene Huddleston photograph. (C&OHS Collection, COHS 1144)

No. 2755 has a train of empties headed up the Coal River Subdivision at Sproul in July 1949. Gene Huddleston photograph. (C&OHS Collection, COHS 1308)

No. 2755 stands ready to take a heavy coal train to Russell, in front of the Peach Creek yard office in February 1955, in the last few months of steam. The loaded trains out of Peach Creek in the post-war era rated either a K-4 or a H-4,5 or 6 2-6-6-2. C&O Ry. photograph. (C&OHS Collection, CSPR 10115.036)

No. 2723 has a heavy train of coal in charge on the Logan Subdivision main just out of Peach Creek in the summer of 1948. C&O Ry. photograph. (C&OHS Collection, CSPR 1497.16X)

No. 2728 has empties at Henlawson, headed for Peach Creek with cars for the Logan district mines in about 1952. Robert F. Collins photograph. (C&OHS Collection, COHS 36732)

In winter of 1952, K-4 No. 2775 is getting an assist from Clinchfield 4-6-6-4 No. 663 bringing its manifest freight into the Elkhorn City yard, which was on steep grade. Here the C&O joined with Clinchfield and interchanged a large traffic. B. F. Cutler photograph. (C&OHS Collection, COHS 5530)

No. 2782 rests at Elkhorn City yard after bring in a fast freight for interchange with Clinchfield in about 1950. The CRR was a conduit for freight between Chicago and Florida routed via the C&O for many years, especially perishables. (C&OHS Collection, COHS 36733)

Coal from Big Sandy headed usually to Russell and got K-4s for power as shown here with 2716 in 1950 near Prestonsburg, Ky. C&O Ry. photograph. (C&OHS Collection, CSPR 2694)

In the distance a K-4 powers a long train of empties headed "Up Sandy" while tracks of tank cars await loading at Ashland Oil's refinery in the distant haze along the immaculate tracks of the Big Sandy Subdivision in 1954. C&O Ry. photograph. (C&OHS Collection, CSPR 10025.318)

No. 2774 is powering the 6-car Louisville section of the FFV (No. 23) just west of Ashland on the Lexington Subdivision in December 1951. Gene Huddleston photograph. (C&OHS Collection, COHS 6166)

A fat freight in charge of 2749 is seen here displaying great exhaust as it passes the water tank at Meads on the Lexington line in February 1950. Not much coal traversed the Lexington Subdivision, but there were four through and one local passenger train each day and several manifest sections headed to and from Louisville as well as four through passenger trains. Gene Huddleston photograph. (C&OHS Collection, COHS 6169)

Providing what must have been a photographer's delight in exhaust (and a fireman's nightmare), No. 2770 is tackling the 2.67% Corey Hill grade as it takes manifest freight between Russell and Louisville. Gene Huddleston photograph. (C&OHS Collection, COHS 1112)

In a slightly less boisterous scene 2753 is climbing the Corey Hill grade in March 1952. Gene Huddleston photograph. (C&OHS Collection, COHS 1289)

Leaving Louisville with Train No. 22, the George Washington, K-4 2759 will haul the train to Ashland where its through cars will be added to No. 2 for their final destinations at Washington, Newport News, and New York. David Oroszi photograph. (C&OHS Collection, COHS 36734)

K-4 2723 rides the turntable at the large Russell roundhouse in 1953. Bernard Rumker photograph. (C&OHS Collection, COHS 5571)

No. 2739 with its coal train takes the siding at L-2 Hudson flashes by with the FFV at the entrance of Russell yard in summer of 1947. Gene Huddleston photograph. (C&OHS Collection, COHS 1154)

No. 2716 is getting coal and sand at the giant 1,000-ton Russell coaling station in July 1945 as H-6 No. 1513 waits in the background. C&O Ry. photograph. (C&OHS Collection, CSPR 57.100)

Unlike many roads, C&O never ran steam and diesels together (except for a short while on the Alleghany SD when diesel-powered trains had steam pushers), so this is a rare photo indeed with 2785 pulling a coal train with ABA F7 units. The occasion is that the diesels had a mechanical failure and the K-4 was sent to rescue the stranded train. Taken in 1953. Gene Huddleston photograph. (C&OHS Collection, COHS 1275)

No. 2704 is seen here leaving Stevens Yard at the western end of the Cincinnati Division (about 12 miles east of Cincinnati) with C&O's hottest manifest freight named for some years, No. 90, "The Expediter," with a long string of refrigerator cars up front. The "CD" was an ideal railroad for the K-4s with lots of fast freight and passenger work, fairly level grades, and very fast track. C&O Ry. photograph. (C&OHS Collection, CSPR 1091)

No. 2711 is coming east with empty hoppers off the Cincinnati Division while a T-1 takes a 14,000-ton coal train west (north) on the Northern Subdivision to Columbus and points beyond. C&O Ry. photograph.
(C&OHS Collection, CSPR 996)

K-4 2704 is scorching the rails with a westbound manifest passing the station platform at South Portsmouth, Kentucky, on the Cincinnati Division across the river from Portsmouth, Ohio, in July 1948. Edwin O. Tufs photograph.
(C&OHS Collection, C&OHS 36735)

The C&O K-4 Class 2-8-4 Steam Locomotive   **71**

No. 2709 is moving at a fast rate of speed given the shape of its exhaust cloud as it moves onto the Northern Subdivision (Cincinnati Division track is seen at right) at Limeville Junction, Ky. It has a fast freight for Columbus and points north and west in 1950. Gene Huddleston photograph. (C&OHS Collection, COHS 1268)

With manifest "Northern 95" No. 2744 charges up the steep approach to Limeville bridge on the Kentucky side of the Ohio River as its train of mixed freight stretches into the distance in August 1948. Gene Huddleston photograph. (C&OHS Collection, COHS 36736)

No. 2722 , with "Northern 93" manifest at Stockdale, Ohio, along the Northern Subdivision in August 1950. Not suitable in power for the heavy coal trains on the Northern, the K-4s were sometimes used to good effect on the fast freights. Gene Huddleston photograph. (C&OHS Collection, COHS 1679)

In July 1946, No. 2717 pauses from its labors at Parsons Yard, Columbus. (C&OHS Collection, COHS 33295)

CHAPTER FIVE

The "Other" C&O 2-8-4s

The Pere Marquette Railway, which C&O had controlled after 1928, was finally merged into the C&O in June 1947. With it came a large stable of steam locomotives. The PM had already begun its dieselization, whereas the C&O had not yet made the final decision. The steam locomotives that came with the PM were given C&O classes and assigned numbers, some were repainted to C&O livery and numbers, while others were not. Many were retired before they were re-lettered/numbered.

The PM's impressive roster of three classes of 2-8-4s, aggregating 39 locomotives, were built in 1937, 1941, and 1944. Some were almost as new as the C&O locomotives. Virtual duplicates to the NKP 2-8-4s, they were close to the C&O K-4s in all regards and could be used interchangeably except that most did not have boosters, whereas all K-4s did. Also, none had cast frames as did K-4s, and most had their sandboxes behind the steam dome.

A number of them were removed from service on the PM lines as diesels began to arrive and were moved to the old C&O lines for service in 1951. One group operated out of Russell, Ky. and one out of Clifton Forge. The engines running out of Russell mainly ran on the Kanawha Subdivision mainline and branch coal trains. In Virginia they handled coal trains on the James River and Rivanna Subdivisions between Clifton Forge and Richmond. They lasted in this service only a couple of years, being among the first to go once the C&O diesel fleet began in the early 1950s.

No. 2697 (ex-PM 1213) brings 160 cars of coal down the James River Subdivision from Clifton Forge at Eagle Rock, headed for Gladstone, where a C&O Mikado will take over for the balance of the trip to Richmond, or possibly the big 2-8-4 will go on to Richmond with the train. Gene Huddleston photograph. (C&OHS Collection, COHS 1273)

On the Pere Marquette the 2-8-4s (known on the PM by their original name of Berkshire and not renamed once they came to the C&O) these great engines had been the priority power for fast freight and heavy merchandise operations were characteristic of the PM's heavily industrialized base of operations (automotive industry).

They received C&O numbers in the 2600 series, just below the Kanawha's 2700 numbers. However, many operated until their retirement still lettered and numbered Pere Marquette.

PM No. 1218, still lettered for its former owner is seen here along the James River at milepost 6 just out of Richmond on June 1, 1952. J. I. Kelly photograph. (C&OHS Collection, COHS 36793)

C&O No. 2696 (ex-PM 1212) headed east from Russell with empty hoppers for the coal fields in April 1951. Gene Huddleston photograph. (C&OHS Collection, COHS 1303)

C&O Class N 2-8-4 No. 2694, formerly Pere Marquette No.1210, with coal train near Russell, Ky. circa 1950. Gene Huddleston photograph.(C&OHS Collection, COHS 35290)

No. 2700, the first of the class, is shown here spruced up and looking like a million dollars at Huntington shops in 1955 before donation to Coonskin Park in Charleston, W. Va. - Like many park engines it declined, was not taken care of, and eventually was given to the St. Albans, W. Va. Volunteer Fire Department, who later sold it. It passed through several hands and now (2013) is stored in bad condition at Dennison, Ohio. C&O Ry. photograph.
(C&OHS Collection, CSPR 3787)

After having been donated to Peru, Indiana, in 1961, No. 2789, the last of the breed, is seen here being refurbished at the Miami County Locomotive Association at North Judson, Indiana in September 1989 where it is currently located .
Bruce Emmons photograph. (C&OHS Collection, COHS 36794)

K-4s Postscript

Afterlife

No less than 13 K-4s were saved and donated to various cities and institutions by C&O's public relations department led by Howard Skidmore, who was very much aware of the importance of the steam locomotive in the history of America. Under him, almost any city or town could apply and get a C&O locomotive. The K-4s were chosen as the main class to donate because most had perhaps because most had lasted to the end of steam and many were still in storage when the program began in the mid-1950s.

The following were preserved, and have listed their whereabouts at this time (2013)

- 2700 - Dennison, Ohio, Depot-Museum, in very poor condition.

- 2701 - Displayed in Buffalo, New York in 1954, later scrapped on site after severe vandalism.

- 2705 - Stored at Russell yard until 1972, moved to B&O Railroad Museum in Baltimore where it is on display.

- 2707 - Donated to Cleveland in 1955; sold for scrap in 1981, but rescued by private owner. Sent to Illinois Railway Museum in early 1990s where it is on display.

- 2716 - Donated to Kentucky Railway Museum where it is currently on display.

- 2727 - Donated to Museum of Transportation, St. Louis, Missouri, where it is on display.

- 2732 - Donated to Richmond, Va., later moved to the Science Museum of Richmond (former Broad St. Station) where it is stored, not on display, and in bad cosmetic condition.

- 2736 - Donated, on display at National Railroad Museum, Green Bay, Wisconsin.

- 2755 - On display at Chief Logan State Park, Logan, W. Va.

- 2756 - On display at Huntington Park, Newport News, Virginia.

- 2760 - On display at Riverside Park, Lynchburg, Virginia.

- 2776 - On display at Washington Court House, Ohio.

- 2789 - On display at Hoosier Valley Railroad Museum, North Judson, Indiana.

When 2716 was given to the Kentucky Railway Museum in July 1956 the shops no longer had stenciling for steam locomotives, so diesel lettering and numerals were applied! This locomotive was later leased by the museum to Southern Railway which painted it to look like a Southern Railway engine, and ran it for two years on excursions all over the east. It was then returned to C&O appearance and taken back to the Kentucky Museum, where it rests today under an enclosure. C&O Ry. photograph. (C&OHS Collection, CSPR 4461)

No. 2705 is seen here in 1953 bringing a train into Handley, West Virginia yard from the west, probably off either the Coal River or Logan district. Overhead photos of steam locomotives are rare, but
are much in demand by modelers. After all, in a model, people often see its top, whereas in real
life, the locomotives and trains are seen from the side or lower. The wide Kanawha River is to the
right. The K-4's certainly spent more time along their namesake than any other.
(C&OHS Collection, COHS 3400)